BLUFF YOUR WAY IN
ANTIQUES

CHARLES HEMMING

RAVETTE BOOKS

Published by Ravette Books Limited
Egmont House
8 Clifford Street
London W1X 1RB
(071) 734 0221

First printed 1992
Reprinted 1993

Series Editor – Anne Tauté

Cover design – Jim Wire
Printing & Binding – Cox & Wyman Ltd.
Production – Oval Projects Ltd.

Grateful thanks are given to André
Launay and Richard Howlett.

Objects on the cover include:
a silhouette, a tin glazed Lambeth
plate, a pewter measure, a 1765 glass
with opaque twist in the stem, a brass
bell with an ivory handle, fish servers
with silver and mother of pearl handles,
a Georgian silver sauceboat and an
under glazed blue printed tea bowl.

CONTENTS

Introduction

To be an accomplished bluffer in antiques means you have mastered the art of not letting others know when you don't know something.

What you do know of antiques is that they should be rare, unrestored, in perfect condition and at least a hundred years old. That is unless you are a purist. Purists hold out for 1830 (i.e. before the Victorian era with its mass production). They will probably continue to do so until they themselves pass the 100 mark and are incapable of stating a preference.

Being a large subject antiques requires the sort of effort that few self-respecting bluffers are prepared to make. The way to get round this is to recognise that which is not antique – to know what to look for so as to distinguish the suspect from the original. In other words to spot the **fakes** and **forgeries**.

A **fake** is an imitation, as instanced by the plastic daffodil. It is generally harmless, legal and frequently though not intentionally, pretty obvious. Quote Eric Hebborn, a master at reproducing old masters, 'Fakes should be enjoyed for what they are rather than questioned for what they're not.'

A **forgery** on the other hand is the plastic flower which purports to have been grown from seed. It is harmful, illegal and doing its best not to be the least bit obvious. As **Rubens** (1577-1640) wrote to a collector referring to a copy of some of his work by a pupil: 'As the reproduction is not yet quite complete, I am going to retouch it throughout myself so that it can pass for an original as necessary ... and regarding some other copies, I have retouched them to such effect that they can hardly be distinguished from the originals ... They are perfect miracles at the price.'

To become a true antiques expert is a study of years. We do not claim to give you chapter and verse, but offer you brief chapters to verse yourself in the bogus versus the genuine article.

Ceramics

Pottery is usually fairly thick and heavy and made to be used. Porcelain is generally thin and light and made to be admired. You can see your fingers behind it if you hold it up to the light. Ceramics is the term for both.

A ceramic should always be approached with an air of confidence. Amateurs are afraid of dropping it. You, however, will convey the impression that if you do drop it, it does not matter because you can always buy the pieces.

Always lift a valuable piece with both hands, placing one on the bottom and one on the top, checking that any lid, head, hat or detachable part is tightly held. Remove any removables. Once the piece is firmly clasped examine it with a knowing smirk, then turn it abruptly upside down and look at the mark. That will tell you everything as there are only about 1,500 ceramic marks to choose from. If they've slipped your mind, grunt, nod and return the piece. If the marks are clear, claim to have forgotten your eyeglass. If an eyeglass is unfortunately available, claim you need your contact lenses to use it.

It is unforgivable to insult collectors (as opposed to dealers) by telling them that the piece you just dropped was not what they thought it was (and paid for), or even worse, was a fake, unless you sound certain.

We are not suggesting you talk of fuddling cups (cups with conjoined compartments communicating internally), made in slipware at Crock Street in Somerset between 1697 and 1770; or that you toss off a remark about a trailed slip posset-pot made for Ralph Toft; nor is it necessary to know pots of potters, but recognition of a few pieces from prime places of plate-making make a good start.

Old English Pottery Slips or What You've Just Dropped

Bristol

Early Bristol pottery is like Lambeth. Late Bristol is like Liverpool. Even professionals are defeated by these three. They all potted from c1680 and made a great deal of Delft ware which was a copy of the Dutch pottery which tried to copy Chinese porcelain. (Just to make life difficult, Delft ware began in Liverpool in 1710.) It is, in fact, ordinary earthenware covered in white tin-oxide glaze to look as much like porcelain as it can. A Bristol (or Lambeth) charger bearing James II's portrait with one eye half-way up his forehead and the other half-way down his nose, in blue, purple and yellow on a white ground is genuine because scores of reproductions have James with level eyes.

Davenport

Heavy, cream earthenware with blue print patterns marked DAVENPORT (often with a little anchor) that shares its name with a small Georgian mahogany writing desk with drawers that pull out sideways. Both appear in reproduction, neither gets woodworm but only the pottery feels like fine orange peel.

Derby and Doulton

Brown, hard, stoneware not decorous enough to attract much attention. Expect to see it full of nuns' raspberry jam in convent shops. The Royal version is more showy but not necessarily reserved for better things.

Fulham

Heavier than Derby, Doulton and anything up to a

hod of bricks, this comes as vast brown or grey mugs with applied relief depicting hunting scenes. Not much is left, which you may think is a good thing.

Leeds
Rather elegant enamelled creamware with pierced patterns like lace doilies. Modern reproductions lack the finesse of originals; if you have dropped one, grovel in suitable form – perhaps making a comparison to a work by John Daniel (see Staffordshire) while you look for your cheque book.

Rockingham
This looks like Leeds pottery with streaky brown gravy all over it.

Mason
This is white earthenware alleged to contain slag, and therefore called 'Ironstone'. Usually blue and red, it has MASON written on the bottom of mugs and plates so you can't go wrong. But neither can anyone else. After 1830 it offers a Chinese style of vases and jugs like vivid pagodas with square panels of Chinese scenes. It all looks like reproduction because it is so colourful, so it is probably genuine.

Minton
The ubiquitous Willow Pattern. Point out that this so-called 'Chinese' design is alleged to be the work of Thomas Minton of Caughley in 1780. Reproductions often have transfer sections which do not quite join up. When dropped, try not to say "Oh well, plenty more where that came from."

Minton were also the most prolific makers of glazed tiles – very decorative and collectable.

Lowestoft

Lowestoft china isn't – and neither is 'Chinese' Lowestoft. It is Chinese china with European decoration exported from China (where else?) so you might like to let that drop too.

Nottingham and Derby

These are indistinguishable from each other to all but fanatics. Just admire the piece and comment on the fact that they maintained their simple design elegance when others became too elaborate. Enthuse about early pottery and porcelain having an 'organic' living quality which later technical perfection lacks.

Pratt Ware

Lead glazed pottery (butter dishes, cream jugs, and lids, lots of lids) commonly in red, yellow, indigo and violet. Also brown, orange, blue and green. Chunky, goggle-eyed portraits of Wellington and Nelson were prominent. Use terms like 'forthright', 'colourful', 'a real Pratt'. Few people falsify a name like Pratt.

Staffordshire

Just about everything could be described as Staffordshire because just about every potter turned and slipped there at some date. There are more reproductions than originals under this name. A charming figure of the actor William Charles Macready as Macbeth was turned out in 1852 and the moulds were still in use in 1962, four companies later, the figure getting smoother and less defined with the years like a jellybaby sucked for a century.

Before you drop any original figures drop these 'Staffordshire' names: **Astbury**, **Adams**, **John Daniel**, **Greatbach**, **Hollins**, **Mason** (above),

Ridgeway, Turner, Josiah Wedgewood, Whieldon and Wood.

Ralph Wood was responsible for the (in)famous Toby Jug (forerunner of the Staffordshire figures) copied by hundreds of potters and now described by many dealers (in private) and most collectors (in public) as a piece of English nonsense. Harry Elwes alias Toby Fillpot was a noted toper upon whom the jug was based. There was also a sort of lady Toby jug portraying Martha Gunn, a famous Brighton bathing beach attendant, which is much more rare.

You can profess a soft spot for these, knowing as you do that originally they were not jugs at all but containers (like the thermos), the removable tricorn hat being the cup. But as most cups got broken or lost later ones are moulded in one piece, hat on head, making the thing quite useless (except as a delicious bit of nonsense to collect). When breaking one say "It wasn't an original Ralph Wood anyway." Unless, of course, it was.

Whieldon produced mingled glazes to make 'tortoiseshell wares' and collaborated with **Astbury** to produce a run of rather simply modelled figures like seated bagpipers in tight breeches with shiny hats too small for their heads, popular for this "naive charm" during the 1740s.

They are a vast contrast to **Wedgewood** finesse. Pick any piece of pottery from green and yellow 'cauliflower' wares to silver lustre, say "Wedgewood" and you might well be right. Or any with the famous blue jasper ground (Wedgewood blue) with white relief figures, cream-white dinner services with black decoration, or tea cups in 'antique black basalt'. Most of these are still in production – by Wedgewood.

Walton
Little rural earthenware figures liberally sprinkled with flowers.

Cadborough
Makers of a Sussex pig – a pottery porker with a detachable head to be filled with spirit so you could swig a 'hogshead' without dire effect.

Porcelain

There are three accepted forms of porcelain: English, Continental and Chinese. Breaking porcelain is even more ill-mannered than breaking pottery, and generally a lot more expensive.

The Great Paste Race (English v. Continental)

The Chinese invented porcelain somewhere between 618 and 906 AD during the T'ang Dynasty, and kept the lead and the process all to themselves for a thousand years. When porcelain reached Europe, potters could only mimic it, until around 1700 when **Johann Böttger** at Meissen near Dresden found it was really a mixture of china-clay and china-stone. This Meissen mix was called 'hard paste' and all china bluffers should know that Continental hard paste porcelain is always German until about 1770 (except when it is Swiss).

Thus the German factories: Meissen (1710), Hoechst (1750), Berlin (1752), Nymphenburg (1753), Frankenthal (1755), Ludwigsburg (1758), and Zurich (Swiss - 1763).

This happy dominance was shattered by the Sèvres chemists of Vincennes, France, who managed to imitate porcelain from china clay and a 'fritt' of powdered glass. But this same 'soft paste' or 'artificial porcelain' had been discovered separately in Britain at **Bow** a year earlier by **Frye** and **Haylyn** who opened a **Chelsea** factory that year, ahead of the French, which just goes to show that first come, first Sèvred.

France and Britain then turned out soft paste until William Cookworthy discovered how to make true porcelain in 1768 and went 'hard', opening factories at **Plymouth**, **Bristol** and **New Hall** (in the potteries) – and the Sèvres team followed suit in 1769. (For the conclusion of the contest see **Parian** ware.)

China bluffers can easily tell the difference between hard and soft pieces with a nail file. If it makes an impression on the base of a piece without great effort the paste is 'soft'. If you have to grind your teeth, blunt the file, and drop the piece from the force, it is (or was) 'hard'. But both hard and soft originals are defiled by Sampson of Paris copies which even put professionals under pressure.

All English porcelain was soft until its hardening off by 1770, so a delightful little pair of (very rare) Bow Monkeys c1757 hard enough to blunt your file on, aren't. The file-bending Chelsea tureen of the c1755 Red Anchor period isn't either. Most English porcelain factories were established during the soft period: 1710 Liverpool, 1737 Lowestoft, 1745 Chelsea, Worcester, 1749 Bristol, 1750 Bow, Limehouse, Longton Hall, 1751 Derby, 1772 Caughley, 1780 Coalport, 1796 Pinxton, 1813 Nantgarw [Nant-gah roo], 1820 Rockingham.

Lament the fate of **William Billingsley**, chemist and china painter, who produced the most beautiful paste in the 1820s made at Nantgarw, Pinxton and

Swansea, until losses in his kilns reduced him to decorating other people's work again. "Oh when one looks at a piece like this, one recalls Billingsley's aspirations."

Limehouse is a good guess under pressure: it lasted about 18 months around 1750 and its pieces are unmarked and so rare that for any unmarked soft paste it is a fool-proof soft option. Say 'Limehouse': few can prove you wrong, and you might even be right.

About 1800 **Spode** perfected 'bone china' — a new 'body' of china-clay, china-stone and calcined-bone or bone ash. This replaced all others and has hardly altered since.

For anything after 1820 bluffers can paste over the cracks in their lustre by commenting on the "satisfaction of technical perfection" but adding that it "lacks the organic beauty the old imperfect pastes possessed."

Chinese Porcelain

Being a millennium ahead of everyone else, the Chinese changed styles in handy 300 year chunks, or dynasties. To avoid certain bankruptcy, nothing pre-Ch'ing should be dropped in any circumstance, except dynastic names.

The Ch'ing period (1644-1912) was one of hectic ferment in Chinese china. There were four colour families in succession, all thoughtfully named in French for the foreign market: Famille Noire, Famille Verte, Famille Rose, Famille Jaune (each being named after the colour most dominant in their decoration).

The great Ming period (1368-1644) is famous because if you tap a piece from it, it goes *Ming*. It works with *Ch'ing* as well.

Parian Ware

Do not make mockery of this 'mock' marble named after the real thing on the Greek island of Paros. It is exceedingly collectable, and still somewhat undervalued, despite its former popularity.

By the 1840s **Copeland & Garrett** (a company founded by Spode) had matured a new hard paste porcelain with a creamy, waxy finish that had more life than the dead-white continental kind. To fill the needs of an eager market it was then churned out by all the main English factories in the form of beautiful, classical female figures, animals, nymphs and shepherdesses, heads and busts which, especially when chipped and bust, look exactly like the marble originals they are copied from.

Pewter

Pewter is very soft and easy to forge. Thus most of its history is about stopping people (mostly pewterers) claiming that it is what it isn't. Pewter is an alloy or metal purée whose essential ingredient is tin with a dash of brass, lead and a zest of antimony.

To ensure the 'good quality of English pewter' and prevent 'unfair' competition (i.e. any competition) Ordinances (1348) were set up to establish that pewter was Sad (beaten) or Lazy. High quality metal, used for plates and chalices, was 'Sad', softer metal was 'Lazy' and used for noggins and 'bendy candlesticks hunched up like ye Quasimodo', and an – unmentionable *very* Lazy for commercial wares and toys – 'sold to persons of no account (ye French) on account of it being soft as putty'. There was much debate about whether spoons were Sad or Lazy. Mostly they turned out pretty Sad.

In 1473 London pewterers became a Livery Company to seek out 'false wares', forfeit them and fine the maker. They spent a happy and lucrative 130 years sending their vice squad round the shires to ensure country pewter stayed really Lazy and Sad. By 1620 the provincials decided they were happier with their own Sadness and their pewter became generally inferior, softer and Lazier. Quality and reputation of pewter declined outside London in spite of being 'touched' since 1503.

A **Touch** is the maker's identity. From 1503 Touching pewter was compulsory so as to discourage wares of ill re-pewt. All Touches were stamped on 'touch plates' in Pewterer's Hall which was burnt in the Great Fire of 1666 and so melted all the Touches. It was rebuilt and re-Touched by the pewterers working since 1640. This means there is open house for a forger fired with the notion of creating a lost 'touch' from 1640 back to 1503, in the hope of a sale to a 'soft touch'. Marks on the other hand denote good or bad quality.

Four Small Marks are a bluffer's gift, often found in addition to the Touch and Mark – usually the initials of the maker, followed by a date (that is when his Touch was registered, not when the piece was made). More initials means a trade arrangement with another maker.

Because it's so soft, age can be added to reproduction pewter by scratching it with wire wool, pitting it with acid, and rubbing dirty metal polish into the abrasions. Bluffers should know what shape pewter things were at certain times to know what they won't be.

Plates had no rim grooves ('reedings') gouged in them until c1670, then two or three until 1710, and one big fat moulded one till 1750.

Porringers (little bowls) belong to the great age of broths and solid things that turned runny overnight. The de luxe porringer of 1550 had two handles like fleur de lys but pressure of porringing meant only one handle by 1650 (super de luxe model no exception). So a two-handled porringer of 1660, isn't.

Flagons pre 1675 were tall, tapering, with bun-shaped or 'Beefeater' lids, then taller with domes and finials and stubby spouts. But York and Wigan made acorn-shaped ones called York Flagons celebrating this dazzling first in North Country design. Except when they made them straight, with long spouts to be Northern. Bristols are tubby, breast-shaped spirit measures made when everyone else's were flat. Often dented, rarely bust.

Tankards appear in plentiful reproduction, mainly in pubs, craft shops and fairs. 1685-1710 they were straight with domed tops, c1730 onwards tulip shaped, unless they weren't. Modern ones usually have no tops.

Candlesticks were generally bedpost shaped till around 1700 then formed like upturned sink plungers after a hard night with the plumber. Modern ones haven't had a hard night.

Spoons usually have six-sided shafts before 1650, then 'knops' called balls, strawberries, apostles and aldermen. Their bowls have the wide end toward your mouth, opposite to today's. You are not likely to find a reproduction with a jellybaby-sized alderman on the end because anyone with the strawberries to do that would forge something more valuable.

Silver

In former days the English, Irish and Scots regarded silver as money you could eat off and drink from; you melted down your dinner plate (known as white plate) in a cash crisis. When solvent once more you got it back as a goblet. Cash-calls were dire during the Civil War, so little pre 1660 English silver survives.

Bluffers need not look for fakes. Forgery requires counterfeiting the assay marks, a criminal offence with many years in jail. (Although 'English Georgian' silver is frequently forged in Italy.) Bluffers should know that in England the golden age of silver followed the arrival of French Huguenots, when Louis XIV revoked the Edict of Nantes because he disliked Protestants called Hugue.

Great Huguenot names to drop are **Pierre Harache**, **Pierre Platel** and his pupil, **Paul de Lamerie**. Before Harache entered the Goldsmiths' Guild (1682) English silver was either tubby and heavily embossed with leaves, fruit and little heads, as if your dinner was welded to the outside of the cup, bowl or porringer; or it was straight and tubular as in flagons, tankards and jars.

The Huguenots having worked in better quality silver transformed dumpy tumblers into tall cups with harp-shaped handles, evolved flagons into ewers, and put graceful curves on everything. Bluffers pressed to comment on this period may use sage phrases from:

The Bluffer's Old Saws Silvernac

Of 1680-1720 silver: "Saw a straight tankard the other day. What would we have done without Harache I ask myself?"

Of tea and coffee pots: "Saw a marvellous **Liger** [pronounced Leezure] pot heating on a **Pyre**."

Of punch bowls: "Saw an astonishing Monteith rim by **Richard Syng**."

Huguenot designs gained credibility over all others in Queen Anne's reign except for the traditional straight plain tankards, much cherished Baroque punch bowls and wine glass coolers, which were gadrooned, scalloped and fluted, chased with cherubs, overgrown with acanthus leaves and thoroughly scrolled to excess.

Of all 1720-70 silver: "Greatest period of English silver. Saw a fine **Adam** salt the other day. Fitting finale. Of course, there's **Storr** in store."

Of cruets: "Saw a dazzling trio of pierced casters by **Pierce**."

Of a candle holder: "Saw an unusual sconce by **David Williams**. So elaborate for such a plain period."

Everything got curlier and curlier (Rococo) until **Robert Adam** who (stunned by Classic pieces unearthed at Baalbek, Rome and Herculaneum) brought classicism to design. So, oval Grecian tea pots, classical sugar bowls, Periclean tea urns,

Olympian soup and Delphic sauce tureens ruled until by 1800 it was all so spare, graceful and sublime that it could not be stood any longer. Vulgarity burst forth lead by the Prince Regent who commissioned Rundell & Bridge to 'build' his silver to designs by sculptors like **C.H.** 'massiveness is the principal characteristic of good plate' **Tatham**, **Flaxman** and **Stothard**. Many fine 18th century pieces were wrecked by 'improvements'.

About this time Birmingham and Sheffield began using stamping presses to churn out fashionable silver. The Victorian construction-kit type silver cobbled together designs of different periods in one piece. Probably the greatest name to remember of the Regency/early Victorian craftsmen is **Paul Storr**.

No five-star bluffer should be seen without an eye-glass. Made of silver it should be found in a pocket, deep down, with difficulty. When the eyepiece is firmly fixed in the eye, the hallmark is examined and a grunt grunted. The eyepiece should then be released so as to fall into the pocket held open with the free hand.

It is now you can venture to comment. "Mary Chawner and George Adams did their best work in that style," will suffice. If the piece was indeed smithed by Chawner and Adams you score 100. If it wasn't, you still score 100 for not having committed yourself to saying that it was. There are about 350 silversmiths whose names you could mention, but naturally, you won't.

Copper

Copper is both soft and tough, which means it is easily worked, but as easily destroyed by verdigris, the blue-green bloom which eats into the surface.

You can tell the copper-bottomed original from the brazen frauds when handles are riveted, not brazed (soldered); and the underside is folded into place with a double-thickness of metal at the joint – not a welded cop-out.

Point out that the surface finish of the genuine article was achieved by hammering the surface until the punch marks were virtually eliminated: they never have the phoney smoothness of young offenders. Explain that real rims are curled over, and honest edges are joined together in dovetails.

Unlike brass, which unpleasantly affects the taste of food, copper shines as cooking pots and pans, and helmet-shaped coal scuttles regularly tinned inside by tinkers – itinerant tinners. Warming pans resemble frying pans with a lid and long wooden handle, a kind of copper-headed lollipop filled with hot coals and used to massage feather beds on cold nights. All copper were ale, spirit and corn measures – wide-mouthed vessels 6"-12" high, with a heart-shaped terminal at the handle base, used to scoop the right amount from a bunker of grain. The seal of originality after 1826 is a lead stamp with the initials of the monarch fixed to all measures once they were standardised.

No true connoisseur could confuse the elegant 18th century copper ale-jacks (jugs) standing on bases 'equal in diameter to the height of the vessel', which bellied out below. By the 1830s the cost of this skill placed them out of bounds, and straight-sided shapes (which could be quickly polished off) took over.

Brass

A marinade of copper and zinc, seasoned with tin, brass was called 'battery ware' in medieval times because it was battered into shape; but serious battering began in England in the late 17th century especially once the beaten French Huguenots arrived fully determined to get at least two brass farthings to rub together. Top brass maker was John Lofting of London, until rival city Bristol (which produced zinc) became the biggest place of brass beating, then (c.1760) Birmingham had the brass-neck to take over.

Chandeliers are the earliest examples of work by known makers in the 1680s and, because it did not rust, horses, soldiers and seamen found themselves buckled and buttoned with it. Bluffers should know the origin of the famous remark. Brass cannon called Monkeys had racks for their iron cannonballs; but in freezing weather the iron contracted faster than the brass racks and the frozen balls fell off the brass monkey.

In no time rolling mills got down to brass tacks turning out vast quantities of candelabra, lamps, ink stands, vases, candlesticks, furniture handles, screws, hinges, casters, statues, gun fittings and shell cases of every calibre.

You could well become brassed-off with the morass of reproduction and faked pieces. Certainly shire horses would each have collapsed under a ton of metal if all the horse brasses sold as 'genuine', really were.

Watch out, for modern brass can easily be aged by a spell in the compost heap to give it that authentic greenish tinge – more effective than chemical faking which bites deep into the metal but leaves it otherwise unworn. Bold as brass, try the fingernail test, for it cannot be scraped off as true patina on old brass can.

Coins

This is not a good ground for bluffers: there is far too much at stake – money. It is far better to bank on the experts' opinions. Let them get it wrong.

When excusing yourself from comment, you may care to coin the tale of the infamous **Billie** (Smith) and **Charlie** (Eaton), two Thames mudrakers of the 1850s, who discovered a genuine medieval medallion. They sold it to the British Museum for a sum which inspired them to make fake medieval 'antiquities' out of lead, and cock-metal (a lead and copper mix) and sell them to the gullible public – a proper lot of Charlies.

In the few years before they were exposed they probably produced around a thousand objects, making innumerable mistakes, such as dog-Latin inscriptions (e.g: dogum Latinus) and Arabic numerals for '1000 AD' centuries before they came into use.

Now that their work is collected, you may speculate on the possibility of counterfeit Billies and Charlies.

Glass

There isn't all that much glass about due to the fact that glass breaks, and most has. You may be fairly confident that little is not what it seems: if tampering is involved, it tends to take the form of grinding down the rim of a chipped glass to level it off, which you may feel is a fairly practical measure.

The first thing to do when you pick up any glass is flick it nonchalantly with thumb and finger till it emits a resonant tone, loud enough for the owner to wince.

The second is to feel the base for a possible pontil [pronounced punty] mark. This is the scar left when the 'ponty', the long iron rod attached to the end of blown glass, is detached.

From around 1790 these scars were polished into a smooth depression, but not always. So, if when feeling the base of any glass, you cut your finger on the sharp edge of a punty mark, you know that it must be an old glass.

Finally you can turn your attention to the glass it is made of. Early flint glass varied considerably in weight and clarity. Make it clear to others that it was **George Ravenscroft** who developed (c1674) what is now called lead crystal, from calcined flints. The following year he used lead oxide instead of vegetable potash as a flux producing a glass cleaner, heavier and softer with greater refractive brilliance than anything previously made. Sadly he died shortly after, never knowing that everything since has merely been to try and improve on his shining success.

There are lots of glasses to break into, snap up and reflect upon. Spotting the **knop**, the chubby decorative blob on stems of 18th century glasses is a pleasurable pastime in its own right.

You can have *ball*, *bullet*, and *cylinder* knops, sharp *bladed* ones placed sideways as if responding to a hard squeeze; *acorns*, *angular,* and *annulated* knops which appear to have been breeding in successively smaller pairs down the stem; *merese*, snuggling between bowl and stem, *quatrefoil* like little bent four-leafed clovers, and *swelling* knops, a slight stem protuberance filled with a welling teardrop.

Bluffers should not be caught knopping in their

ignorance of the **twist**. This wound its way within glass stems from about 1740 and blossomed in different varieties like a climbing vine. First shoots came in the form of the *mercury* or *air* twists with bubbles blooming end on end like beads, or budding at tearful intervals.

About 20 years after came *opaque white* twists, single like barleysugar, or plaited double or treble around each other, some as intricate as lace; these *mixed* twists finally flowered red, yellow, blue and green in spiral rainbows – quite enough to send you round the twist.

Cut glass (as opposed to cheaper moulded glass) can be *facet* cut (to glitter), *hollowed*, *incised* and *engraved* (see Jacobite).

Some fun can be had trying to recognise particular kinds of antique glasses, such as:

cordial glasses, like tiny Victorian lampposts, 6" high with little bowls on long stems;

dram glasses, also called nips and joeys;

ginettes, thick glasses with little bowls for gin;

goblets, which hold a quarter pint or more in big bowls on shortish stems;

ale glasses, long narrow flutes for long ale thirsts;

romers, pale green glasses with spherical bowls cut off at the top like deformed goblets (but not after 1825);

rummers medium-size, resilient glasses with large ovoid bowls, short stems and small feet (1760-1850) but plenty still exist to take a shine to, and, rather more rare –

Jacobites, political glasses which bear the cryptic engraved emblems and mottoes of The Cause. Look out for the six-petalled Jacobite rose with one or two buds. The rose represents the House of Stuart, the small bud, the Old Pretender and the large bud, his son Bonnie Prince Charlie's arrival in Scotland. Other Jacobite emblems include a stricken oak, an oak leaf, a bee, a butterfly, a carnation, a daffodil, three ostrich plumes and a thistle. In other words, you could attempt to convince someone else that any glass bearing some sort of design is Jacobite.

Scrimshaw

The molars, incisors, tusks, and ivories of large, luckless marine mammals were enthusiastically inscribed by sailors to while away the hours at sea. These could either be hollowed out for things like tobacco pots and small flasks, or left solid as ornaments.

Anyone wishing to collect such pieces should be quick to realise that no amount of etched teeth could supply 20th century demand, so any scrimshaw they might fish up are more likely to be dentures.

It was two Brighton sharks, disaffected dentist's assistants, who first had the idea of making casts from originals and then faking them from dental cement. Note that fake market stall scrimshaw has a milk-white, powdery appearance like smooth Polyfilla and goes *clunk* when its lid is tapped against its body. Bone is creamier, lighter, and goes *clink*.

The other tooth test involves sticking a red-hot needle in the base of the suspect scrimshaw and waiting for the smell of burning ivory. You will be unlikely to get it: cement doesn't burn.

Netsuke

Bluffers should speak of 'netski' (Japanese for toggle) when referring to these little ornamental pieces, mostly carved from ivory and occasionally from cherry, ebony and persimmon.

You should know that their great period was the Edo, pronounced briskly 'eh-doh' (1615-1868), and their main function was to secure waist cords which passed through a hole or notch in the netsuke. You will also know that they feature animals, especially the rat which is the symbol for wealth, or many little domestic characters, like pot-bellied potters.

After lamenting that Western styles of dress in Japan meant they fell into disuse, sum up by observing that virtually no signed netsuke now exist whose signatures are incontrovertibly genuine. Then advocate hot-rodding (the Scrimshaw test) since much netsuke for sale today is moulded in epoxy resin.

Small Arms

Handguns are like clothes: functional objects which sometimes become works of art. The oldest, rarest, and most inefficient are more art than weapon. The phrase 'lock, stock and barrel' meaning the complete outfit comes from the three most important parts of a gun being brought together – 'the whole shooting match.'

The Lock

This is the crucial working part of the gun. Pay close attention, it is the part most often forged. To determine the period you need first to appreciate the types.

The older and more inefficient the lock, the more valuable.

The **Matchlock** (1480-1620), the earliest, needed a lighted match on an S-shaped lever flicked by the trigger in order to fire.

The **Wheellock** (1620-40s) was so expensive it was only supplied to élite troops who wouldn't panic when it jammed or 'hung fire'. It didn't last long.

The **Snaphaunce** (1640-1650s) a flint held in a hammer ('cock') striking a steel so sparks flew into a small 'pan' of black power whose cover shot back so the main charge exploded. There was an even chance of hitting a moving target with this, if it didn't 'go off at half-cock'.

The **Flintlock** (1650-1850). With the steel and pan cover merged into one, serious carnage was now possible. Cheaply made, even a simpleton could use it. He could also get 'a flash in the pan', the false start when the flint sparked but the gun didn't fire.

The Stock

The stock is the gun's wooden body. Musket butts stayed much the same so you need only take heed of the varying shape of pistols.

Bluffer's Pistol Butt Guide:

1620-70: butts have a flat, cut-off look;

1680-1730: butts grow large swellings (pommels) on the end, metal butt caps with fierce little heads and long metal spurs up the butt sides;

1730-50: pommels shrink but keep their fierce
shrunken heads;

1750-90: pommels disappear and butts get to look like
small hockey sticks.

So a wheellock with a big round butt pommel is a
marriage for money and you should seek an annulment.

The Barrel

The barrel was made by a specialist, like famous Mr
Durs Egg (a Swiss in London), who hatched various
beautifully crafted 'cocks' as well: a bad Egg is rare.
Just remember the musket has a longer barrel than
the pistol and you hold it with two hands instead of
one.

The commonest antique shop musket is the 'Brown
Bess' or 'Birmingham Gas Pipe', the Tower Musket
which armed the British infantry from 1720-1850. A
really ambitious squaddy could get off four to six
rounds a minute into trees, poultry, mules, buzzards
and even the enemy with this. It got shorter as it
grew older, with barrels of 46", 42" and 39", so the
longest is the earliest and rarest, and if a 39" Brown
Bess has a 1750 Tower stamp on its lock plate, someone is having a barrel of laughs.

By contrast the long-barrelled, superbly crafted
hunting gun made for the squire (which cost him
more than a dinner service) with walnut stock,
engraved barrel and silver mounts, took fourteen
movements and a minute to load, then hopefully shot
a partridge lulled into a false sense of security by the
rigmarole. These now sell for as much as a minor

French Impressionist's painting.

A peculiar kind of barrel is that of the musketoon or blunderbus, the most popular household weapon for centuries. Very short muskets with flared muzzles to make a louder bang, they were used in the country for scaring intruders. Their muzzles were trumpet-like early on, narrower later, as presumably hearing improved. There is no truth in the story that they fired old nails or broken glass, simply a shower of little lead balls like sheep droppings.

Shorter barrels in the form of pistols come in 14" long 'horse' size for use on horseback, slightly smaller 'target' pistols for inanimate objects and even smaller 4-6" 'travelling' ones, often with two barrels one over the other, kept in pockets, ladies' muffs or if you had thin legs, down your boot. Owners shot themselves more often than other people with these. According to one (short-lived) cavalier wit "horse pistols were used by the horse as he made a better marksman than his master, to shoot other horses which made a bigger mark than their master."

Pairs of good ordinary round-barrelled target pistols are often deviously passed off as 'duelling pistols' (which command high prices as they are matching pairs of precision craftsmanship). True duelling pistols have heavy, frequently octagonal barrels and the butt is gently curved to fit the hand in the aiming position. Superbly engraved (e.g. *tremor mortis, morte pejor*' – the fear of death is worse than death) they commonly have two triggers: the second a 'hair' or 'set' trigger, adjustable to go off at the least touch to compensate for any unfortunate wavering while squeezing.

The percussion mechanism, (a cap like a tiny copper top hat full of fulminate) replaced the flintlock about 1850. It was vastly more reliable so thousands of flintlocks were converted to it. These converted weapons are fairly common today and generally fetch lower prices, so some dealers put the flintlock back claiming it and the gun grew up together, when of course they have just met at a dealers' party and become good friends.

Never a flintlock either was the antique Enfield rifle-musket of the Crimean and American Civil War, and its successor, the much rarer Martini-Henry breach-loader of the Zulu and First Boer Wars.

An important repercussion of percussion was the successful revolver. Rivals for forty years were Sam **Colt**'s American manually cocked six-shooters (sumptuously engraved examples – one decorated with a stage-coach hold-up along the barrel – which he presented at London's 1851 Great Exhibition now fetch between £8,000 and £15,000) and the three automatic-cocking British-made **Adams**, **Webley** (the most powerful revolver of the age), and **Tranter** (liked by women for its short barrel and double triggers for thin fingers).

Percussion guns of the late 1800s are on the margin of being antique and some, like the Colts, are still in (limited) production. They are rarely forged, but no enthusiast should call the bluff of any century-old gun, especially if it comes with its trousseau of moth-balled ammunition. Get it test fired or your last effects may be auctioned along with it.

Edged Weapons

Heroic cutlery is plentiful and highly collectable. It is not forged so much as altered, which can affect its value. Fakes in edged weapons concern divorce and marriage and you have to recognise the correct partnership.

For instance, an elegant English 18th century hilt can be joined to a fine 17th century Spanish sword blade because the later owner had a larger hand, and the value may enlarge proportionately.

On the other hand, a blade engraved with the name of the great Spanish swordsmith 'Sahagom', topped by a worm-eaten handled hilt with two bent iron hand guards is definitely due for a separation.

It is important to recognise that swords *are* the blade. The hilt is normally an accessory while the blade was where ancient warriors believed the sword's spirit dwelt. Old blades could marry pretty young things that wore gilt wire, jewels on their pommels and sometimes twisted silver quillons for the wedding.

Edged weapons divide into six powerful families, whose members changed shape over generations. 'Let your sidearms be shorter as your arms grow longer', an 18th century squire advised his son, 'most ladies detest...a scabbard so long it raises or cuts their skirt.' Bluffers should know that the oldest swords have the longest blades (usually). When the average duelist was 5' 5" his sword was barely 1'6" shorter than he was. But generations later a 5'10" Regency buck was content with a coy 2'8".

The **Rapier** family is long, willowy and elegant, designed by Spanish Toledo steel couturier c1500 so that Frenchmen could shout 'En Garde! Fleche! Parade! Reprise! Reposte! Touché! Balestra! Appel!

Ah – merde! at each other. The **Dish-Hilts** are the most numerous antique members of this exclusive family around today.

Longest and oldest family (of pre-medieval origin) are the **Two Handers**, up to 7' long, but weighing as little as new-born baby, the **Bastards**, shorter with hilts big enough for one and a half hands to hold, and the **Claymores**, 5' long with a hilt like a crucifix. Bluffers should know about the sword-fraud in connection with the latter; the name 'Claymore' is used by dealers and Scots romantics to describe the much smaller Basket-Hilted Broadsword, which is no relation and was not born in Scotland.

Most numerous in antique shops is the **Broadsword** family, the dominant group known as the Baskets after their steel and brass basket-shaped hilts. Their more elegant cousins the **Sabres** (some slightly curved, some straight) were still being used on horseback in 1918. Cavalry were still disputing the best way to use them about the time they got armoured cars.

Foreign visitors, the **Scimitars,** often appear on restaurant walls. They may impersonate Indian Mutiny veterans, but were generally born in Calcutta c1970. Those seeking the most expensive accommodation are the **Samurai**, with aristocratic 13th century blades married to gold and enamelled hilts, attended by silver and ebony scabbards, hoping for a £150,000 settlement at Christie's.

Aged members of the **Small Sword** family, little brass-hilted spikes like fire-pokers are a mite bigger than the **Socket Bayonet** or **Lugger** (a member of the Dagger fraternity) who when engaged to a Brown Bess musket, via a ring round her muzzle, becomes more valuable as a devoted couple than in an unattached state.

Prints and Watercolours

The bluffer will declare, like the best art historians, that the greatest English contribution to visual art is water colour painting. From about 1780 to around 1840 everyone from campaigning generals to picnicing school girls produced water colours (or WCs) just as they would take snapshots today. Never was so much painted by so many, and later equalled by so few.

Among the most celebrated names are Thomas **Girtin**, Alex 'Blotmaster' **Cozens**, David **Cox**, Thomas **Varley**, Peter 'Hayricks' **de Wint**, the four **Cotmans**, J.P. **Bonnington** and J.M.W **Turner**. The first four are known for their romantic landscapes, the others Norfolk, coasts, towns and Turner painted everything, everywhere, generally better than everyone else, often working back and forth adding details to each wet picture while others hung on a washing line to dry.

Water colour pigments are notoriously 'fugitive', i.e. they change tone and fade away, particularly blue which goes to grey. They also suffer from various skin conditions which affect their price:

Sunburn

The water colour's complexion is sensitive to strong artificial light and tans in direct sunlight. It may also get hair-line scorch marks when the glass has been cracked or broken at some stage but the picture not immediately removed.

Dishonest back street doctors replace faded colour with new paint washes which can leave a crinkle where the new wet patch touches the dry surrounding area. To avoid this they dampen the whole picture, but the older colours then 'shift' slightly like an out-of-focus photo. Proper re-touching has a dilute gelatin solution put over the surface and then the colour stippled on with the point of a nearly-dry brush.

Freckling

Speckles of mould grow on iron particles in the paper. They can be removed by a sensitive solution of bleach: a delicate application to the back of the afflicted areas with a cotton bud or brush, restores the patient from these unsightly signs of ageing.

Jaundice

Respectable water colour paper is made of rags and sometimes forced to share its frame with a mounting board of undesirable character made from cheap acid wood pulp. It catches the cheap board's bad habits of going brown or yellow as chemicals migrate, and has to be bleached to return it to health.

Acid Ingestion

This causes paper to fray and crack up. A remedy is neutralisation by brushing a Wei T'o solution on to its back after the paper has been lightly rinsed, dried and warmed.

Many hypochondriac water colours can be caught by the astute bluffer who takes an interest in their case and achieves a reduction from the dealer in view of the patient's condition.

Water colours are sadly only too easy for competent forgers to counterfeit. Using old paper supplied by endpapers from old books (or staining paper with a solution of dilute tobacco, or even smoking paper over a damp wood fire) and the contents of a Georgian or Victorian paint box (full of porcelain pots containing original pigments) can take the result back 150-200 years quite comfortably.

One of the clues to a pretence between an elderly paper and a pensionable pigment is that water colours usually only have a skin-deep affair with paper – they stain only a little way below the surface. Old paper is more porous and newly wedded colour will embed itself to quite a depth, even showing at the back if you can gain access. This is more marked if modern pigments are used on an old paper.

More cunning and almost impossible to detect is the counterfeit signature, the only art in this being to match it with a picture similar in style to that of the artist whose signature is to be added, and adding it.

Prints

There are a number of different kinds of print that you should be able to distinguish without difficulty.

Woodcut
The upmarket version of the potato print, you can refer to this method as 'relief process'. In woodcuts the wood is hollowed out around the design, ink rubbed over the raised areas, and the print made from the result.

Wood engraving
'Ah,' you should say, 'intaglio'. Here the ink is held in grooves or dots (as it is in etching, steel engraving, stipple, mezzotint, drypoint and aquatint) incised with a sharp tool, and the block is pressed against thick paper to create a detailed image of depth and

delicacy. The greatest of English wood engravers was Thomas Bewick in the 18th century who pictured everything from the private life of the cuckoo to the private life of the cuckold.

Etching
The source of many an seductive invitation, the design is cut in wax laid on a metal plate for greater delicacy than engraving straight into metal. When the plate is put through a roller press it leaves an indentation on the paper all around the picture – the plate mark – the easy way to distinguish this from an ink drawing.

Line engraving
Here, a design is cut straight into metal with a graver which leaves a 'burr' (a metal sliver) that is removed with a scraper. Victorian steel engraving pictured everything from the *Charge of the Light Brigade* to ladies' corsets, John Martin's *Belshazzar's Feast* with bolts of lightening and cringing sinners, being sold by the thousand for drawing-room walls.

Dry Point
This is the art of reproducing double vision without the drink. The 'burr' is not removed so it leaves a fuzzy effect around the engraved lines. Like a hangover the burr wears of, so dry points (much favoured by Rembrandt) are rare and expensive.

Mezzotint
With this method the metal gets a good roughing up and the bits that aren't intended to be hold ink are smoothed. The result is a delicate bruising of greys,

and velvety contusions of black. Romney and Sir 'Sloshua' Reynolds produced copies of their oil painting this way to keep themselves in claret.

Stipple engraving
From 1750 masses of little dots were cut in the wax of the etching which give the picture a superb softness of effect. The most popular exponent of this in England was **Bartolozzi**, but probably **William Wynne Ryland**, engraver to George IV, was the finest. Unfortunately his greed surpassed his versatility: he took up forging stock certificates, and was the last man to be publically hanged at Tyburn.

Aquatint
A way of achieving immensely delicate gradations of 'water colour' effect in black and white, which was often then given a pale colour wash. Goya and Turner used this method, Turner once leaving the initials of his engraver, Charles Heath, on a beach barrel in a print of a sea storm because Heath had just gone bankrupt and was 'washed up'. **Baxter** (1804-67) pioneered 'colour printing' rather than coloured prints by using up to 20 acquatint blocks, each in different colours to build up one picture thus earning an impressive price even from the first impression.

Prints suffer from the same ailments and skin complaints as water colours, and can be nursed in the same way. The bright bluffer should recognise plain originals which have been heavily made-up: prints were coloured immediately after printing and the paint stayed on the surface of the paper. But an old uncoloured print that has been newly tinted will have absorbed the stain like blotting paper.

Silhouettes

These were named after Louis XV's finance minister, Etienne de **Silhouette**, who paid only for bare essentials and no details – and was thus cut out for the job.

Be quick to point out that the English had already produced work like this some generations before, only they called them 'shades'. Then elaborate on this technique of "catching a shadow" in which the cunning use of lamplight and lens produced a tiny profile which could be outlined in pencil on paper, then blacked in, or cut from white paper and mounted on a black background.

A shade more ambitious, they might be half or full length, with a landscape sketch behind; or women could appear lamp-back in profile but with hair of gold, or gold hair ornaments, sometimes on the rear of an oval, convex mirror. **Isabella Beetham** committed shades to glass, while **John Miers** enjoyed the highest profile as an artist. You can also draw **Mr**. **Buncome** into the frame as master (from c1745) of figures in coloured clothes and black profiles.

These shades were all hand-work, and inevitably the 19th century produced a silhouette machine which traced and blackened the sitter's character in $2\frac{1}{4}$ minutes. Here the famous names are **Edmund Frazer** of Derby and **William King**, while postage stamp-sized profiles for ring bezels and brooches by **West** helped him to keep his finger on the pulse of portrait fashion.

The silhouette basked in success until the advent of the Daguerrotype (which pre-figured photography) cast its shadow over them – a case of who Daguerres wins.

Furniture

Artists and craftsmen of earlier centuries were quite blatant about duplicating the styles of bygone periods, with or without devious intent. The greatest faker or 'reproducer' of all, the illustrious **William Morris**, whose main claim to fame (in furniture) was to mass-produce the traditional Sussex rush-seated ladder back chair (in stained oak with front and rear stretchers, of course), which explains the pained expression of his wife Jane who had to pose on it. Customers would have found it difficult to distinguish from its 18th century forebears.

Anyone in the antiques trade could tell you that nothing in wood is ever what it seems. But as long as the purchaser is happy, no-one is likely to rock the late Georgian mahogany dressing table (with ebony and satinwood classical inlay motif and early Victorian cabriole leg replacement). The marquetry line between restoration and outright forgery is a fine one. Some furniture in constant daily use may have been repaired several times during its life; resplatted, re-covered and even re-designed with no dire intentions. But restoration of a single leg to a **Hepplewhite** shield-back chair may reduce its ultimate value.

A set of six Hepplewhite shield backs is going to cost you as much as a BMW, but a set of eight, which is far more rare will cost you double that. Thus a single damaged chair with two good legs and a number of usable splats are mated with two new chairs to make up the handsome set of eight. This pair of fillies out of Old Stringer by Shield Back are very difficult to identify on the auction course when running with the field.

There are few things less lost than the cabinet makers' 'forgotten skills'. An under-cover company of cabinet makers could make you a **Chippendale** chair from scratch when the right price is offered and Chippendale's ghost would not know it from one of his own. In fact many of today's 'antiques' are made in India and dealers can order complete sets of **Sheraton**, **Hepplewhite** and so forth in good mahogany for a very reasonable sum. It is up to you to spot their lack of age or the greater light-ness of touch of the originals.

The Victorians, who did everything to excess although with matchless panache, produced more, and frequently better, reproductions than anyone else. Only the most astute dealers and hawk-eyed connoisseurs can tell some Victorian reproduction Georgian or Queen Anne from the original, and as the mid-Victorian repro piece is itself now aged about 130, it is a collectable antique in its own right.

The Victorians used a wide range of woods, often light softwoods stained dark to simulate mahogany or ebony as well as the true heavy hardwoods, and a surprising amount of their juggernaut furniture is crinoline light. Bluffers should know their woods, for those who ask a dealer "Shouldn't this drawer be lined with oak?" may receive an evasive answer if it should be and is not, but they will receive nothing but polite contempt if it already is.

As a ready reference, here are the popular woods of the main furniture periods:

Table for the In-Grained Connoisseur

Tudor (1485-1603) – Oak

Jacobean/Carolean (1603-1649) – Oak, Elm

Restoration (1660-88) – Oak, Walnut, Beech

William & Mary/Queen Anne (1689-1714) – Walnut (with Ebony chips)

Georgian/Regency (1714-1830) – Mahogany, Ebony, Rosewood, Satinwood, Beech, Maple

Victorian (1830-1901) – Mahogany, Ebony, Oak, Walnut, Beech, Maple, Birch, Pine.

The budding connoisseur will notice that the three great woods of this furniture parliament, Oak, Walnut and Mahogany, are the 'front bench' or 'cabinet', the others being decorative 'back-bench' members for contrast, inlay and marquetry. There are also some constituency workers like Pine or Beech or Elm who act as supports but rarely receive premier attention.

Oak

Everything in England, from ships to wooden legs was made out of oak until Charles I lost his head on a block of it. After that the trees ran out but for one Royal Oak left for Charles II to hide in.

Oak is usually coffee-brown in colour with a close grain, resembling a slice of roast beef with paler streaks scattered like fat in the meat.

Tudor furniture was all made from solid pieces of oak which allowed for very little carving typified by their huge Trestle or Refectory Tables with vast bulbous legs to support big-bellied Tudor appetites.

The Jacobeans added the Farthingale Chair (a stool with high broad seat for women with broad farthingale dresses); and Charles I a Gate Leg Table (a round table with folding flaps) specially designed to collapse when you cross your legs.

Walnut

With the arrival of walnut from the continent where it was à la mode for well furnished courts, furniture became lighter, smaller and decorated. Walnut is the easiest of woods to recognise: a deep amber colour with darker whirling swirls, daubed with knuckle-sized cauliflower-shaped mottles.

Great furniture firsts of the Restoration: Charles II Chairs (with cane seats and exuberant S-shaped scrolls flanking their back-panels), Carolean Day Beds (long versions of the chairs for horizontal discomfort), Pepsian Bookcases and James II Dressers were made in oak as often as walnut. But by Queen Anne's time chairs – especially the Queen Anne with padded drop-in take-out seats, hooped-shaped backs with a violin-form centre piece and cabriole front legs with ball and claw feet – were almost always in walnut.

So was the Queen Anne Grandfather Chair, the high-backed winged easy chair (mass-reproduced by the Victorians), and the Queen Anne Dressing Table, walnut veneered and copied by everyone.

Mahogany

Usually a deep henna-red hardwood, mahogany replaced walnut (c1730) as the craftsman's dream. A wood whose superb patina improves with age and polishing, mahogany captured the furniture market. Look for a decorative grain of dark red and umber streaks, or sweeps like ostrich feathers. Brick hard it does not crumble when carved, so **Thomas Chippendale** encouraged chip and dalliance of it and succeeding craftsmen spent seventy years blissfully balling and clawing it. Chippendale's comrades in the mahogany brotherhood were **William Kent**, **Robert Adam**, **Henry Holland**, and his own son, young Thomas.

At this time the gentry sent their sons on Cook's Grand Tour of Europe, and the famous names were publishing a grand tour of cabinet making: **Sheraton**, **Hepplewhite**, **Ince** and **Mayhew**, **Mainwaring**, masters of furniture design. All made their own screws by hand. They went on doing this well into the Regency period, making the Grecian Couch, the Drum and Pillar and Claw Dining Table, and the Canterbury (a drawer on wheels with a rack for sheet music) with which young ladies could entertain company while Mama poured tea from the Teapoy (a tea-chest on a tripod table with brass and rosewood inlay).

The **Yew**, a dense wood of glowing golden ambers (patterned with dark brown configurations), is slow growing so in short supply, and the English **Elm** yields a golden wood patterned like tide ripples on wet sand. Most of London's architectural furniture – bridge piers, wharves, piles, sewers – were built of Elm, but you can also see it wrapped around a long-case clock of the 1700s with its pale gold surface stained to bring out the wood's mass of browny-black flecks, like quill-pen ink splats.

Beech resembles freckled skin with a light gold tan and was as plentiful in the 1600s as oak was in the middle ages, so Restoration craftsmen decided to make use of it. It has been the flesh, skin and bone of much furniture ever since.

The haute couture cabinet of the 1700s wore ebony, rosewood and satinwood. **Ebony** arrived from the tropics to strike a black note in furniture before it reached harpsichords and ended up in the *Ebony Concerto* via the piano. Queen Anne legs have occasional veins of it to set off the walnut kneecaps where it resembles strips of liquorice among the walnut whips. Much lighter wood like pine was 'ebonised' especially in the Regency or 'Empire' period, which means it was stained black.

Rosewood is named after its fragrance, usually applied in veneer sheets, but sometimes a solid piece like little Regency gaming tables. Either claret red with a rippling burgundy grain, or a rosé with darker streaks like sediment swirls in wine, you can lean forward and 'nose' its bouquet.

Satinwood is a literal description for choice glossy timber that resembles Champagne-coloured watered silk. Used in larger sections, **Maple** and **Burr-maple** was a decorative convenience for de luxe commodes in lieu of walnut. It is pale gold with a pattern like bent drawing pins.

Birdseye maple (a disease affecting the skin of the tree) was used for objects from wall panels to little Victorian love-letter boxes with mother-of-pearl inlay and brass locks to keep secrets intact. Birdseye resembles the little brown speckles on a thrush's breast, like – a bird's eye.

Known as a 'weed-tree' by foresters (because it is small and invasive), **Birch** was too soft and friable for furniture and its bark was worth more than its bite except as prison punishment. But on small decorative boxes and in veneer strips it has an iridescent quality, looking like shoals of velvet tadpoles swimming in syrup.

Pine was used for things other than Welsh Dressers, but not for furniture you *discussed*. The Welsh discussed dressers but as no-one else spoke Welsh, this didn't count. And when you saw pine you didn't know it, because it was painted not to look like pine.

Great Distress

This is the technique of giving recently-made 'period' furniture a hard time. All the knocks, bruises, scratches and stains supposedly sustained over a century or two are inflicted on the wood in a few minutes with bicycle chains, knuckle dusters and knives; candle grease and ink being spilled in the drawers for good measure. Instant dirt and grime (a coat of black wax,) a little sandpapering, a few stains and a worm hole or two (if the piece is stored with infected logs to convalesce) complete the treatment.

Distressing is highly effective but fortunately easily overdone. Most forgers get carried away – forgetting to soften sharp corners but gashing a surface that is not much exposed; pitting the side of a dresser but leaving the top of a cutlery draw smooth when 200 years of table knives would have snagged it.

Zipping Up

The opposite of distressing, but with equal purpose to deceive is 'zipping up' – making a piece more exotic. Old cabinet makers would inlay different bands of marquetry in intricate designs on to flat surfaces; or leave the wood plain and patinise, i.e. use a special varnish layer upon layer to give a luminous quality of different hues.

To imitate these techniques restorers frequently get calls from dealers to 'Zip this piece up a bit.' Zipping up makes it easier to ensnare the customer, and includes:

a) cutting in some cross banding (an inlaid band of wood whose grain runs in a different direction
b) putting in some stringing (a thin line of veneer)
c) insetting a floral marquetry design.

Detecting phoney inlay is hard: be suspicious if the piece seems strangely 'clean' – rather too crisp, with no mellowing where the wood meets the contrasting surface especially if other areas appear old and worn.

Altering

The observant buyer will scrutinise the construction of any piece of old furniture. Movement of drawers causes grooves to be worn into the framework over a long period, but a recent model will not have these scars. Also look out for new nail work in back panels, the filling-in of old nail holes, and sharp edges where the panels have been replaced by equally sharp practice.

Clocks

There are three types of clock for bluffers to watch for: table or lantern clocks, bracket clocks and long cases. Face lifts and transplants are common and some cases remarkable. The English, who were often behind the times, imported their clocks until c1600. As these were weight-driven with a spring mechanism and intended to hang on a wall they should have been called bracket clocks, but carried from room to room were dubbed table clocks instead. They had only one (hour) hand and lost at least quarter of an hour every day.

In 1658 the pendulum swung into use, after which the English didn't lose a minute and bluffers may affirm that London clockmakers led the world until they failed to move with the times after 1860. **Thomas Tompion** with 550 clocks and 6,000 watches to his name carried the most weight in English clock work, with a workshop just over the London boundary to stop the clockmakers guild chiming in on his success.

These new time-pieces were called bracket clocks. They should have been called table clocks because they usually stood at the bedside or on desks, not hung on walls, but early bracket clocks had usurped their name, a timely piece of English logic. At first they had engraved brass faces, then silvered ones, and lastly white-painted iron with black numerals.

Minute hands arrived in the early 1700s, with second-hands a close third. Pendulum table clocks were wound every 8 days via two keys in the face: so older clocks had two fake key-hole beauty spots painted on to look more up-to-date. Longer pendulums meant slower ticks, so less winding, a timely movement leading to the long case clock or a case of long waits between winding (1-6 months). One of their best makers was **Chime**, of course.

BUYING ANTIQUES

There are four chief types of antique shop, and different bluff manners are not only appropriate but will also be practised by the dealer in each.

The Country Town or Village Antique Shop

This is rarely called Ye Olde Antique Shoppe and if it is, you are not likely to find anything genuinely antique in it. If you do, it is because the owner has not yet had the chance to sell it to another dealer.

The shop might be called, say, Centenary Antiques (contents up to 100 years old, just), and the proprietor buys genuine antiques (and good repros). He or she is successful because they practise SPQR (small profit quick return) or they have perfected the gentle art of buying their stock cheaply and can then mark it up 200 per cent.

Behind the genuine 18th century pewter tavern pot containing a bunch of fake flowers (water drips will mark the early Victorian oval side table with late Victorian claw feet) there is often a young man or woman who is a top antique dealer-to-be. They pick up items from the weekly country town auction, household clearances, country house sale and antiques fairs (*q.v.*).

They top these up with the odd item from the local market stall dealer. That is why the bluffer will never find a genuine antique on the village market stall amid three copies of *War and Peace* Vol 2., fifteen *Illustrated London News* (1935) and a pile of Pyrex dishes and plastic toys. If one was ever there Centenary Antiques bought it before the stall opened, which is the reason the stall didn't open and the owner is in the pub.

Other items are bought from the amateur antique dealer on the edge of town (who is also worth a bluffer's visit), who has less money and no business sense. From him – it is invariably a him – Centenary Antiques will unearth chipped rummers for £2 from beneath a collapsed Chesterfield, which lost its stuffing when it fell off the roof of his rusty Renault 5, or brass candle snuffers for £5 each from behind a peeling Victorian wallpaper screen. Later they will return for the screen, possibly pay him £60 for it, and charge you £800 after getting it restored for £300.

The owners of Centenary Antiques are usually very charming. If you take something to be valued by them they will tell you what they would offer you for it, and leave you to work out the mark up from that. Then they will try and sell you something they have not been able to shift by suggesting that someone of your taste and aesthetic sensibilities could make something 'wildly improbable' out of it.

The Home Counties Antiques Shop

This is mostly found nestling up to the Real Cream Teas Room and the horse-brass encrusted beer-out-of-the-wood pub, opposite a bank and building society in a Kent/Surrey/Sussex/Berkshire town square.

Behind the reproduction 17th century pewter tavern pot with real flowers atop a reproduction 18th century gate-leg dining table you will find a fierce female of any age. She is fierce because she does not know very much so does not want to be asked. You are supposed to know what you want, if it is there and if you like it. If it is and you do, you say "Good afternoon. What a charming Welsh dresser/Canterbury/piece of Bristol porcelain/enamelled snuff box", write a cheque and depart with a wrapped object (any larger purchase will arrive 3 months later, if you are lucky).

By placing a dragon to mind the shop the owners have astutely prevented any haggling via embarrassing questions in a sharp hand of call my bluff. The owner is always 'out'. If you buy a reproduction here assuming it genuine, that is your problem. They did not say it was genuine. In fact, they did not say anything at all.

So unless you know your marks, knurls and knops, go to Harrod's where first class reproductions are sold as such without the surroundings suggestive of the real thing.

The Antiques Showrooms

The informed and wealthy who never carry cash and employ someone else for the heavy work of writing their cheques for them, shop for their antiques in distinguished emporia in Knightsbridge, Kensington, and Mayfair. No passing bluffer who puts a foot into these establishments would call them 'shops'. Only a regular client would use the term as a form of endearment, much as Yehudi Menuhin might call his Strad a 'fiddle'.

The bluff here is to look as if you can afford to be on the premises at all. If you are male wear a hat and remove it. If you are a woman wear one and keep it on. Everything here will cost you a second mortgage so do not touch anything or breathe too loudly. Never ask the price of anything: obviously you can afford it if you want it, and if you cannot afford it, you have no business being there.

Note that the Georgian silver cigarette box is not for sale; it holds cigarettes for reliable customers, and no purchase will be wrapped but sent to the address on the card you are expected to proffer as you leave.

The Faded Frontage

There are certain shops (usually found on approach roads to cities, e.g. London's Harrow and Fulham Roads) which appear from their fronts to deal in antiques but do not. Inside there is the front of an empty long case clock, the front of a commode (wormed, 1903), the front of a stringless cello, and an individual who is probably fronting something going on upstairs.

The Antiques Supermarket

This is what happens when an enterprising young person buys a warehouse, store, church, etc. and partitions it to make as many cubicles as possible, renting each of them for as much as possible. Each 'stall' is hired by amateur dealers with no capital to buy a shop, or by professionals who have a business elsewhere and want to sell some stock to new faces.

Bluffers should recognise that many of the items here are younger than the people selling them: 1914-1918 Great War British helmets (from Taiwan c1988 supplied for movie extras), Harry Roy 78s, etc.

The would-be connoisseur should not confuse the Supermarket with the Antiques Hypermarket, which is for the jet-set collector on a business trip who pops

in to pick up some Meissen birds between flights.
Everything in these is truly Antique, i.e. before 1830.
Centenary can get a better price here for its little set
of Nips and Joeys picked up at a quiet country house
sale. You will see the serious money on holiday here,
but you do not have to wear a hat, or remove it.

Antiques Fairs

Here the top dealers meet, usually in the ballroom of
a local 5-star hotel – to show each other and wealthy
collectors their best pieces. The Purists view with
patronising grin the Victoriana and Edwardiana
while secretly collecting the latter because in 20
years' time they will have run out of pre-1830 English
antiques to ship to America.

Auctions

The Country Town Auction

Most country towns hold auctions once or twice a
month, generally in places called The Produce Market
or The Corn Exchange. On auction day it is full of
1930s fat-encrusted fridges, old Singer typewriters
with arthritic keys, rusty cast-iron lawnmowers built
like Sherman tanks, and very occasionally a little
piece of genuine Minton which everyone has assumed
is repro, or an early Victorian sampler of a sailing
ship with utterly unworkable rigging in a mahogany
frame, which great aunt Matilda made for midship-
man Albert after her visit to Cowes of 1836.

Any of these will have been spotted by the local

dealers by dawn's feeble light. They would have offered the sampler ship owner £400 for it straight off her wall knowing it to be worth at least £600 and possibly £800, but her son who has never been interested in anything older than he is, has foolishly put it all into the local market. Dealers can believe their luck, because dealers' luck is founded on the bliss of others' ignorance.

The Household Sale

Suburban semis in big towns do not usually yield much to the magpie dealer eyeing for shiny antiques but the average 1930s villa can sometimes hatch a good brood of memorabilia: an old 1950s chrome-plated tea cosy-shaped radio, a great black Bakelite telephone with teminus letters on its circular dial and bell like a fire alarm, the occasional 1948 Utility three-piece suite, a horsehair-filled masterpiece with a massive square back and a box of war-time 'Very' tissues lost down one arm.

If a true antique should by chance expose itself dealers will pounce and cover it with bids. But these are better memorabilia shows for bluffers who do not get bitten by the bidding fever and prefer a little bit of faded period charm. The dealers will snatch the phone and the radio and leave you to find the tissues.

The Country House Sale

The death of a large country house is announced, like a person, in the national press, and its epitaph is the auction. Aspiring bluffers should go to the viewing, which takes place over one to three days and displays the contents for sale, in one to three days, depending on the number of Lots on offer.

The house will be full of dealers, locals who have never had the chance of a good snoop, members of English Heritage who would have liked to see it delegated as a conference centre, and restorers who would have liked to re-gild the ceiling and re-marble the dados if the money had been forthcoming.

Fine Georgian furniture (excellent cross-grain inlay) and dubiously re-upholstered Victorian drawing room chairs stand under a slightly cracked oil of a successful Naval entrepreneur of the Seven Years War, who took 47 ships and built the house with the proceeds. His son on his right (smaller canvas) looks rubicund with good living, his pale tubercular daughter on his left (smaller canvas) founded the library. A genuine **Richard Wilson** hangs over the mantelpiece, and a genuine art historian hangs around beneath it.

In the servants' quarters under the roof there are rooms still stacked with bolts of uncut damask, brought down in Lots. An entire scarlet and blue Crimean uniform (dress and undress) comes down with it, two bullet holes in the left arm. The kitchen was modernised in the 1930s and a Bakelite radio crouches amongst Victorian churns.

The entire contents of the house will be sold. Some dealers are determined to get 75 per cent of it to America, while an elderly gamekeeper wants the leatherbound telescope he's always admired since he was a boy. He hopes it won't go over £20.

The dealers weave between the Lots. One group of them, gathered around a *Times* (foxed, 1815) are not discussing Napoleon's activities but the Regency Sofa Table (mahogany with lyre-shaped supports having arched stretchers). They are all members of a Ring.

Calling the Ring's Bluff

The Ring is a dealers' clique dedicated to ensuring that everything it is interested in can be acquired for less than it is worth. Even the best bluffer is but a novice compared with the Ring. The forger at least misuses real skill. But these trade criminals practise a gamble against each other at the expense of the innocent.

Impromptu matinée Ring performances are given to acquire the piece, so that if you enter an object for auction valued at £1,000 you will be lucky to get £300 for it. The Ring members who have bought it between them then bid amongst themselves for it in an evening performance over drinks.

The Ring has only one great weakness: greed. You can obviate it by diligently finding out what an object is really worth. If you are bidding for it, go up to that price, but never above it. If you are selling, put a reserve price on it. But choose your auction with care: your price may be too high for some small town venues and you may find yourself having to cart your own piece home with you.

Auction Houses

Leading London auction houses don't talk about the year's trade. They refer to it as 'the Season' as if you partake of a stirrup cup and cry "Tally ho!" when a fine hunting canvas is spied running in from the Shires. You can find out what they get up to because they each publish a glossy, fat annual hardback review weighing as much as a sideboard, featuring their best auction kills in sumptuous colour, with information on these and others which didn't get away. A bluffer's bible.

On no account attend an auction with a nervous twitch. You could end up buying Jimi Hendrix's gold lamé trousers for the price of a new car. But the ambitious should attend one at some point in their career. There is no weight compared with the gravity of this precision mime. Only the auctioneer speaks from his high rostrum. The piece is raised (if possible) by an assistant, displayed, and then set down in view. The value (a starting price) and brief pedigree (if any) is recited, and the audience invited to begin indicating its interest.

Some bids come in by telephone: from the Arab who is journeying between his homes; from Japanese who want to fill half an hour usefully between buying up California or selling New York. Other bids are run up by the auctioneer 'off the wall' (that is, conducted with a non-existent bidder at the back of the room so as to keep the price rising). Get as close to the wall as you can: that way no-one, real or imagined, can bid where you cannot see them.

The London houses are masters of the auction world and other hounds concede that they deserve to be. This is because they are prepared to risk their reputation and make a decision. It is important to appreciate that these experts are simply making informed judgements. Their lives are haunted by the one they missed, or the one they mistook, and expertise is hedged around with doubt. This is exemplified by phrases used when advertising items for auction (sale) in their catalogue. For instance:

The Christian name and surname of the artist – In our opinion a work actually and wholly by the artist. Honestly.

The initials of the Christian name(s) and surname of the artist – In our opinion a work of the period when the artist was painting, which may be wholly or partly by him, or maybe not. Take your choice.

The surname of the artist only – In our opinion a work by the school of this artist, or one of his followers, or not by any of these but in his style by an artist who thought it more saleable that way.

'After' followed by the surname of the artist – In our opinion someone who shall probably remain nameless has copied the work of the artist.

'Manner of' followed by the surname of the artist – In our opinion a work executed by someone or other at a date later than the style of the work might suggest.

Bears signature or Inscribed – Someone has signed it and it might or might not be the person who painted it. Any suggestions?

Attributed to – In our opinion probably a work by the artist who painted all, or at least a good part, of it. The less good parts might be by other people or the artist on a bad day.

Circle of – In our opinion a work by the artist's drinking cronies who were less successful than he was.

Markets

London's out-door markets are enormous fun and well worth visiting. Just bear in mind that nothing is worth more than you are prepared to pay for it.

Brick Lane – 'The Lane', Sundays: 4.30 am - 1.00 pm

Good for budding bluffers because the public to dealer ratio is 1:1. The first vans 'pack out' (unload) before dawn surrounded by dealers and dealers' runners with torches. You start with tat, especially on the 'fly' pitches at one end of the Lane and end at the main market, among the junk yards.

Tools, clothes, books, packaged food genuine antiques and semi-antiques lurk. There are hardly any fakes here. Who fakes junk?

Bermondsey – Fridays: 5.00 am - 1.00 pm.

The professionals' market. Dealers dominate all-comers 4:1. Container loads of antique furniture are shipped to the Continent from warehouses in Tower Bridge Road. Dealers descend on the silverware at 6.0 o'clock.

500 stalls and two covered markets deal exclusively in antiques. Five-star bluffers can practise here and four stars can seek promotion. Others should accompany an experienced bluffer or a dealer, eyes peeled, mouths shut and hands in their pockets.

Camden Lock and Stables – Saturdays & Sundays: Lock 8.00 am - 5.00 pm; Stables 6.00 am - 5.00 pm.

The public outnumbers the dealers 8:1. Craft objects, rummage – prints, books, pictures, jewellery, objets d'art, and occasional small genuine antiques gather here, getting topped up from Brick Lane when it closes.

Portobello Road – Saturday: 7.00 am - 4.00 pm.

2,000 stalls in the road and in covered arcades engulf the shops. Dealers outnumber the public 2:1. There are many high-grade antiques, especially prints, silver and ceramics. The place to get '60s when '50s memorabilia is passé. Abundance and utter disorder.

Camden Passage (no connection with Lock or Stable) Wednesday: 7.00 am - 2.00 pm; Saturday: 7.00 am- 5.00 pm.

The average quality rises sharply and serious bluffing is imperative. At Wednesday's market dealers outnumber the public 3:1 but small stalls and polished wares still yield bargains and have not yet engulfed the shops with their protective grilles and Chinese vases. The covered market sports up-market ceramics and silver. On Saturday public and dealers are 1:1. and the place still remains an almost tat-free zone.

The Fiddle

Dealers do more trade between themselves than with private customers (us). Their prices are calculated to make a necessary profit with the trade, but there is always a chance of getting that bit of extra profit with the public, so the higher price is quoted.

Once they make it known they are 'trade' they are quoted the price less 10 per cent, sometimes more, depending on how many favours one owes the other.

You should know that to be 'trade' simply means you buy antiques to re-sell. Whether you do so that day, within a week, or ten years is irrelevant. So there is nothing to stop you calling yourself 'trade' except not wanting to be associated with the dealing world.

If you think you can convince a dealer that you are trade, you deserve the 10 per cent you will then earn. So approach the stall with an air of contented curiosity, as if you already own whatever it is, but just want to be sure it is where it ought to be.

Survey it in your own time. You will want to know the trade price, but don't ask it. Pick up the object, inspect it and put it back. Don't respond to any overture on the part of the dealer, other than a nod.

Then make as if to walk away, half-turn, and ask "What've you got on that?" When told, return a few steps and reply "Doesn't leave much", implying that there would be little worthwhile profit on re-sale.

The haggle then begins:

a) Enquire "What's the best you can do?"

b) If the dealer thinks you're trade he says "Twenty quid to you."

c) Reach in your pocket for your 'wedge', a fat wad of folded ten pound notes. Do it like John Wayne loosening his six-gun. Check through your wedge with your fingers (twitch your lips as you count).

d) Half peel a couple of notes off the wedge and say as casually as you can "I'll split you."

e) If he agrees to meet you half way the performance is complete. Award yourself five stars and reward yourself with another object.

THE AUTHOR

Due to an accident of geography, Charles Hemming was born half-way up a mountain in Wales, but grew up in Bristol (see hard paste Porcelain). He was forced to serious bluffing at school where he spent 13 glazed years and registered with various marks. His parents would have run an antique shop, but unfortunately, they had to work.

Eventually packed out at Goldsmith's College, London, he studied traditional ale measures (by volume), ground his own paint pigments, made fake marble clocks as big as sideboards and long case clocks the size of teaspoons, covered himself in plaster of Paris, got plastered in Paris and professionally veneered in art history.

Finally zipped-up with a Fine Art degree, he began painting pictures ("after" himself, see Christie's) for various galleries, gilding, restoring painted (i.e. fake) marbling and decorative wood graining for country houses (see Auctions), and creating trompe l'oeil to commission (all challenges still welcome).

In 1985 he published *Paint Finishes* about decorative paint techniques, followed by award-winning books *British Painters of the Coast and Sea* and *British Landscape Painters* about the foxed, faded, famous and forged (see Watercolours and Prints).

He is currently Lot-numbered as reserve decorative artist to the National Trust and, (see Ceramics), held in stock at Pratt Walk, Lambeth.

THE BLUFFER'S GUIDES®

Available at £1.99 and (new titles* £2.50) each:

Accountancy	Maths
Advertising	Modern Art
Antiques	Motoring
Archaeology	Music
Astrology & Fortune Telling	The Occult
Ballet	Opera
Bird Watching	Paris
Bluffing	Philosophy
British Class	Photography
Chess	Poetry
Champagne*	P.R.
The Classics	Public Speaking
Computers	Publishing
Consultancy	Racing
Cricket	Rugby
Doctoring	Secretaries
The European Community	Seduction
Finance	Sex
The Flight Deck	Skiing*
Golf	Small Business*
The Green Bluffer's Guide	Teaching
Japan	Theatre
Jazz	University
Journalism	Weather Forecasting
Literature	Whisky
Management	Wine
Marketing	World Affairs

These books are available at your local bookshop or newsagent, or can be ordered direct. Prices and availability are subject to change without notice. Just tick the titles you require and send a cheque or postal order for the value of the book, and add for postage & packing:

UK including BFPO — £1.00 per order
OVERSEAS including EIRE – £2.00 per order

Ravette Books, P O Box 11, Falmouth, Cornwall TR10 9EN.